NON-FICTION RESERVE

This book is to be returned to non-fiction reserve at Headquarters.

It is not to be added to stock at any branch

PURCELL, S.
Fossil Unicorn

Please return/renew this item by the last date shown

Poetry by Sally Purcell

THE HOLLY QUEEN
DARK OF DAY
LAKE AND LABYRINTH

Sally Purcell

FOSSIL UNICORN

ANVIL PRESS POETRY

Published in 1997
by Anvil Press Poetry Ltd
Neptune House 70 Royal Hill London SE10 8RT

This book is published with financial assistance from
The Arts Council of England

Designed by Anvil
Set in Monotype Plantin Light
Printed and bound in England
by Arc & Throstle Press, Todmorden

ISBN 0 85646 282 9

A catalogue record for this book
is available from the British Library

THIS BOOK BELONGS TO SIMON

ACKNOWLEDGEMENTS

Some of these poems have appeared in the following publications: *Acumen, Agenda, The Brazen Nose, Outposts, Poetry London Newsletter, Swansea Review, The Other Branch* (Leamington), *Verso* (Lyon), and in *Completing the Picture*, edited by William Oxley (Stride, 1995).

CONTENTS

January 10, 1984

Like a river of smooth stones the broad road flows
down to dusk unending, stagnant shadow-pool,
and the locked gate where one ice-cold lantern burns.

Branches clash in a dry wind; the twisting path has
    left him
far from landmarks where we could meet,
wandering in the wood of Celyddon.

Easter

Your palace in this world
lay between earth and open sky,
adorned with sun, rain, wind; you saw
into death's glass beehive, knew by heart
the invisible city guarded by skulls
that glint along ramparts & under gateways.

You realised God's pattern
linking all the gardens;
you gave your will entirely
to the terrible journey
out beyond all sea-marks –
to a new grave of clean stone,
home-coming.

Receding into mist...

Receding into mist, the burnt fields
carry their scars towards oblivion
& begin to grow new flesh, in secret;
the cold white honey
that embalmed Alexander
piles up in every cell.
Autumn is an island
in the subterranean sea,
its air patterned by bells
            that melted long ago,
its coral or granite ready to perfect
this time an enduring image.

On Propertius IV.7

'Ghosts are something; death is not the end of all;
a sallow image escapes when the pyre is out.
I saw her bend over my pillow when
she had just been buried by the growling road,
& sleep had gone to the funeral
as I roamed the icy kingdoms of my bed.
Her hair and eyes were still the same,
her dress all scorched down one side;
the fire had gnawed the ring she always wore,
and Lethe's acid had just bitten into her lips.'

That ghost of a ring haunts me more
than all the vampire bitterness
that will not let her die.

'And you shall find all true
but the wild Iland'

Ariadne regains herself & her solitude –
all she betrayed to the stranger
is vanishing as the black sails dwindle
and he goes forward to found his town.

Where salt-star & rose of sulphur
glitter on the rocks at noon
she has her realm again,
making tiny mazes, Troy-games,
with white pebbles in the sand.

The scapegoat Old Year...

The scapegoat Old Year hobbles out
from the westward-facing door
that has opened at last;
time & grief swirl in like the tide
melting a sandcastle.

Drive out the Winter King,
lord of sour pomegranates,
with a weight of dark knowledge
bound to his shoulders –
nail his shadow to a tree.

He is the grain flung out to die, the fool
keeping safe in his wizened heart
what the green hazels know.

He turns from the narrow isle...

He turns from the narrow isle of liberty
where he still wears a crown
and flings into the night
where our world thins to a razor's edge
and there may be no more sea.

Beyond lies the bare path
of rejection of images,
through the broken water, into completer darkness,

       'and a song I tell to no man
unless he sail with me'.

Landsmen for an old crime...

Landsmen for an old crime
condemned to the sea and wind,
we are borne by our shapeless path
into the final storm's eye
through autumn's rain of blood,
or, one moon-freezing night, cast up behind the castle
where God keeps the door like a servant,
with its iron keys in his opened hands,
where nothing more is necessary
and the road
         disappears

Out from time's tumulus...

Out from time's tumulus,
     the black bonds laid on Cronos,
Our Lady comes walking
     with a dish full of light,
light that flows through her fingers,
     waves, ebbs & returns,
between wandering walls of shadow;
     Maria, gateway to the great sea,
draws near
     like a sound growing clearer,
bringing together at last
     the holly-berry sun
& pearls of mistletoe.

15th-Century Woodcut

At the sign of Time and the Wild Man
the World lolls & drinks their house wine
beneath an ever-burning bush.

Just outside crenellated cardboard walls
hangs on a hill Scarecrow Skeleton,
whose rags flap & shrivel in the blue-black wind.

Grey flames roll & drum...

Grey flames roll & drum around this island,
Jack Frost leaps & shakes his quills,
cuckoo-spit glitters – wizards' weather
hangs a net before your eyes.

You must wade through dew and cobwebs,
through a dance of green mounds
(shifting always, looking almost alike),
and seek in vain unmisted sight,
until time dies in your arms.

Dr Dee

Stone, pure as it left His crucible,
is hidden still within each grain of dust,
where we can never come;
break the skin of a dewdrop or mercury bead,
the secret flees to a remoter place.

Since the keys of Eden rusted into a blood-red clod,
we snatch or forge
moments when that world shows through,
the innocence it has never lost
– before 'it is gone, with a brightnesse'.

Linquenda Tellus

Castle, bridge & fountain,
familiar human print on stone & water,
brief houses of the heart

suddenly turn into a grim Little-Ease;
the forgotten voice of ocean
has drifted this far inland.

And without a word, the inland man
turns, to receive his journey –

a lane with shining walls will curve at last
down into that sea of light,
real home & only rest.

Moor, mound & crag...

Moor, mound & crag
rinsed clean of meaning
by starlight,
now you have lost your familiar look
I can leave you,
bury my gems of glass,
start walking into the cold hours,
sure to meet before death's dawn
a cross of wind with arms of darkness,
waters that leave a taste of ice.

Tomis, December

When the numbness wore off and I realised
I was here for life,
I started to thump on the doors of my tomb,
rattling, shouting *Let me in, damn you!*
But they would not open. I stare
down at my bruised knuckles:
Far from home – easily said,
mooed in a maudlin ballad,
but here it cuts like the north wind:
'adrift in a sea with no harbours,
to die on a shore with no name.'

Can there be any future in this blank place,
on the rim of the recognisable world?
Its water, food, soil, air corrode me quietly;
no healing grows here except in my memory.
He spared my life with a view to this dying.

If my shade, or any thing that is me,
escapes the bonfire's crunching jaws,
it will have to wander among hostile ghosts
over this last promontory of earth –
delicate cruelty, that.
Let me return, one day, a small pot of ash & bone,
let me not be exiled everlastingly
from the great lost City;
leaving her was my first and hardest death.

In dreams I fly over my ruined house,
roof & door gaping in moonlight;
I wake and grief stands before my eyes
like a colossal granite god.

Do I need to suffer more?
Somebody thinks I do. My wounds are raw
and somebody wants to pull them open again.
But only a fool insults a grave
or tramples on a rag of shadow.
Hector was a royal enemy
living; the thing Achilles dragged in the dirt
was not Hector; and I am not
the shape crouched in a freezing hut
under a sky like filthy snow
gradually forgetting the sound of its own language,
gradually forgetting trees, grass, birds, the light
of the sun

Poem for Lent or Advent

Signs and shadows
have been gathering reality
as they rush upward
to the surface of time;
they break
into our minds' air, snatch us through
knowledge of the visible,
through the game of images,
into that Love
Who sawed both cross and cradle
out of the same tree.

Merlin's time will return...

Merlin's time will return
    on the swirling tide of grace
as heavenly wind & water reveal
    all stone to be ephemeral.
Easter is a fiery golden tree
outlasting the fresh rains of April,
green candles with a blue flame.

A small wind is fidgeting...

A small wind is fidgeting round the stair-well
the red moon has turned her horns downwards
your candle has quietly made a winding-sheet
madam said to come and fetch you.

At the door of Castle Mirror
spirals on lintel & threshold
reel in a spider-thread of sound,
prepare an invisible net;

skulls glow softly along the wall,
lapped by lime-green fenland,
forever barren, the last wrong turning.

After Crinagoras

Caves in the nymphs' holy headland,
spring water flashing down rocks,
little wooden shrine
           to Pan of the Pine-tree,
gratefully I add a stone to your cairn,
green island in the shadow of God's thought,
        and travel on.

I'll sing you seven seas...

I'll sing you seven seas,
Green skull upon the shore.
What are their memories,
Green skull upon the shore?
Quick sand & dead sand,
False dawn & cold horizon
Ever opening, never closing,
All the wrong cards in one hand,
Which evermore shall be so.

Elizabeth of Bohemia

The sky shines like water above a lake of snow
where a formal garden repeats itself, jarring
into parody, leading to a shapeless fire;

hell-mouth waits peaceful, not content, not impatient,
in the lee of cavernous winter arches.

Rational skeleton in the green tomb...

Rational skeleton in the green tomb of spring,
will your meditation on one abiding word
ever quieten the heart?

                   – Never till it can rest
in its natural home, no longer wondering
if the summer flowers will be early this year.

Be not afeared...

Be not afeared
                    nor confident
when the dragon seems dead,
a handful of brown scales on the ground.

If he has gone to his own place
it is to soak up strength
from crusted pools of bitterness
below the world;

every moment may just have been
his nadir.

The rain...

The rain
is a stranger's
footstep in the porch –
some Hyperborean or Inca
that walks on feathers or fine linen,
some dreamer
who has left his body

The wind
is his hand on the latch,
bringing a gift
or a ghost's knowledge

The darkness will be his face

Out from the moon's hillside...

Out from the moon's hillside
they drift across our noon-day,
chill the April sun,
rap on windows of dream.
They are forgetting how they ever
lived under this air.

And I can scarcely recognise
grief, now levelled by the tide
invading upland gardens,
the fierce immortal sea.

My heart that wanders in your forest...

My heart that wanders in your forest
under the shadows of changing day
sleeps where love like starlight spreads
a colour unknown;
brightness falls like the dust of snow,
to your spring has come the once-wild heart.

Breathing the golden darkness...

Breathing the golden darkness
that is their element,
plumed & leafy creatures glow
deep in a forest of tapestry.
A sudden sting of glittering rain
would wake them into our unquiet air
with a shock like love,
irretrievably.

Lie gently in...

Lie gently in
your natural harbour,
my bones the
breakwater,
your heart
the moon's
reflection;
tears divide
light into colours –
emeralds
       through the fine rain.

Autocrat of the subtle underground world,
he sits waiting for Orpheus the beggar
to scramble down ankle-breaking scree,
past luridly lit waxworks,

and savours the breathing man's pain,
twists & turns like a piece of jewellery
that almost possible condition...

But can the god know what gift he is giving,
that silence for a theme?

Sestina for Two Voices

We slip round the corner of your mind's eye,
Creatures of lonely twilight between hills,
We are never unmistakably seen;
If living men have strayed on to our path,
Our visitation is like that of love
And follows them into their deepest dream.

Where light & shadow variegate the dream,
Leaves of magic trees have dazzled your eye
With every brightness that waits upon love,
Inward-glowing light of enchanted hills,
By which you recognise the coiling path
Which you have always known but never seen.

Then how to understand what you have seen,
Never sure you have glimpsed outside a dream,
Where what you cannot see is the true path?
Is it full clarity within your eye,
Is it the view from frightening hills,
The joy of sight at last made clear by love?

When this light is the beginning of love
It is like nothing I have ever seen;
It is no view from any frightening hills,
It is nothing I have known in a dream,
But it overmasters my dazzled eye,
Commands by knowledge of an unknown path.

I feel that there is darkness on this path,
And I can guess the darknesses of love;
There will be need for me to trust an eye
Familiar with things I have not seen;
There will be times I hesitate to dream
And times when I am frightened of the hills.

I shall not be rejected by the hills
Although I many times will miss their path;
My journey will take me into that dream
Because my guide will always be my love;
I give myself to what I have not seen
Because all knowledge comes not from the eye.

Gold light streams down hills in Apollo's path;
labyrinths of dream lead at last to love;
and fullness is seen by one perfect eye.

After Amairgen

I am the quiet fruit in your hand
I am the green weed that sways in the current
I am the dark red wrack
That clings to ocean's floor below all tides
I am shell or fossil that can strip no further
I am driftwood after its voyaging
I am the sunlight flickering on these pages
Who but I knows the exchange of sea & shore?

As the wind of springtime touches her...

As the wind of springtime touches her
she is transformed, Chloris turns to Flora;
flames of roses run over the earth
which till then had been all one colour.
Time returns; there are no tears now
except to weep for sweetness of love.

Spider...

Spider
      walks up sloping or vertical air
Swallow
      slashes a woven invisibility
Fish glides through soft heavy glass

How are we to believe? there is no scar
and every day ingrains
distrust of sight, of innocence –

Then love, moving in the mind's element,
shows again the clearness unbroken,
and all questions are at peace.

A deep-sea fisherman hauls up...

A deep-sea fisherman hauls up
a sprig of heather with bees upon it;

his coracle skims the top of a wood,
rides over a flowering meadow;

in that world contradiction is unknown,
resurrection has never been needed.

Starting out from the latitude of Byzantium...

Starting out from the latitude of Byzantium
Pytheas leaves that tideless world,
blue crystal globe –

Truth in the map's lighted circle cannot rival
regions of unshaken twilight, solid whirlwind,
rocks that wander invisible,
golden stone oozing from trees;

'The unknown must be there,' he murmurs;
'feel how it wrenches the known.'

Robert Kirk

He has been taken into his book,
out of ordinary time, the copy,
into the original;
and our world's end may leave him unscathed,
beyond harbour lights & human boundaries,
raking through shingle on the penultimate beach
for fossil unicorn.

Shadowless Air, Unchanging Season

Proserpina's garden, ropes of
    scarlet & leaden purple berries
as earth breathes in its dream,
    a snow-cold spring wells up through gravel,
    spreading into stillness
the rocks give off a heavy light
    thick as white honey

    And I have been
    all these things
    in clearings of a forest
    where Time is unknown

Valentine

All night
my heartbeat
scans your name

Along
the rivers
underground

Darkness
love's hidden
Pactolus

Holds in
deep caverns
the ripe sun

At night the snow is blue...

At night the snow is blue,
    reflecting a single eye,
waters above the firmament,
    colour that is alive.

Unravelling threads of rainbow
    return into the sun,
leaving a grey scratched mirror, now
    sealed like a stone.

Meaning has drained away as flood-water sinks into furrows,
Parchment & bone dangle creaking from a green gallows.

Wind-Scattered Leaves

remote as the gnarled | roots of the sea
as a heartbeat soft | & close & strange
a well where stars | all noonday shine
where the mind's eye | is slowly drowning
shadowless depth | swirls across the sand

Aeneid VI

His journey into death & prophecy
has taken, exactly, no time –

the cavern's eye blinks once
and he is back on the beach
          where the ships have not moved.

Remember
clear & still the sleeping shore
in these last moments before dawn,
before Aeneas can bring history.

Wyatt

Darkness like water has filled the hollow garden
where fragments of a drowned face float illegibly;
one yellowing elder tree hugs evil dreams;   .
this lake obeys no moon.

You learned the lessons of the moon
by heart, engraved on darkness;
shape-shifter, true to herself immortal.
Repeating 'But once I was' locks you into the past.

Do leaves imprinted in a jewel's past
live in her memory? Do you?
Take your tide into changefulness now,
from hands that offer bread –
                                        and golden chains.

Seven Horizon Poems

I

Horizon means the thing you never reach,
but see, & long for, never touch;

dancing in a glittering net it parches
heart & eye & salt-wearied throat,

always an enchanted
telescope's range away –

like birds we peck at painted
varnished paper fruit

II

based on Fernando Pessoa

Far-off austere coastline
Leans to meet the ship coming in
With trees in which Distance has no share;
Nearer, the land opens in sounds & colours:
Disembark, and there are birds & flowers
Where, from afar, was only the abstract line.

All the possible shores have vanished; now
This is merely earth & water.

III

That cold colourless line,
seen once before, perhaps,
always almost remembered,
may hold lands that occupy no space,
may widen out into a crack that leads
to the true flower or tree
                or bird
                or fountain,
the last cape of this world,
Apollo's primeval orchard.

IV

A polished steel vizor
is the ship's horizon, a prison
that goes with us unchanging,
makes it hard to believe in movement,
mockery to believe our eyes.

V

translated from Lorenzo the Magnificent –
probably written in the 1480s

A wandering bird leaves its beloved shore
that has grown cold, and flies across the sea

... on every side waves, water, weariness,
nothing else to see, nothing else to feel,
no rock or branch to give a moment's rest

If a ship comes ploughing through the waters,
the sailors may be crueller than the storm...

I hover hesitating in this world

for when the mind has left its native land
confusion is the only thing it finds
and when it longs to seek for shores unknown
it ends in waves of doubt & weariness

Palinurus, clawing at the cliff-side,
dragged by his heavy clothes,
numb & sick from the brine,
realises the god has not lied –
he is going to die on land:
the wreckers crunch towards him
                    with their boat-hooks.

VII

Smeared with weeds & clay,
stung by sand & gravel,
Prometheus wades ashore
on to this island world,
carrying a precious thing –

brazier of rubies
        from ashes of sunrise,
tenderness in his great hands

that for our sake will be nailed to blackening rock.

Cranaë...

Cranaë,
    dark island
where first we lay
on warm grass
    & lavender,

        timeless, touches
        every moment,
colours every breath of common air.

To Thomas Cavalieri

Below the surface of raw stone
the hand's obedient eye can see
the shape that will grow into life
as the scales are prised away;

Snakes fray against a rock
to escape from their dying self
that quietly breaks & blows away,
emptied of colour & meaning;

And in your sudden sunlight
my old skin lies in heaps about your feet.

NOTES

9   *Celyddon*: The magic shape-melting wood that is the northern boundary of this world; see also the marvellous line by Alun Lewis, 'Or Celidon the hollow forest called'.

20   *Dr Dee (1527–1608)*: Astrologer, magician and mathematician.

13   *'And you shall find all true but the wild Iland'*: from Beaumont and Fletcher's *The Maid's Tragedy*, II.ii.73.

15   *'and a song I tell to no man…'*: from the anonymous sixteenth-century Spanish *Romance del infante Arnaldos*; reference to A. E. Housman, *More Poems* 45.

21   *Linquenda Tellus*: 'You will have to leave the land you love…', Horace, *Odes*, II.14.

23   *Tomis*: the grim place on the Black Sea to which Ovid was banished; much use of *Tristia* III.

28   Crinagoras: *Palatine Anthology* VI.253.

30   *Elizabeth of Bohemia*: daughter of James I, who was married to the Elector Palatine in 1613, and as part of whose wedding festivities *The Tempest* was probably first performed. The poem refers to a strange and sinister-looking engraving in Frances Yates' book *The Rosicrucian Enlightenment*.

41   *Amairgen*: poet who uttered the first poem spoken in Ireland. See A. and B. Rees, *Celtic Heritage* (Thames and Hudson, London, 1961) p. 98.

46   *Robert Kirk (?1664–92?)*: a Scots Gaelic-speaking minister who wrote *The Secret Commonwealth of Elves, Fauns and Fairies* (c. 1691) about the Good People and their world, and the times it touches ours. As Yeats says, 'It is very near us that country is, it is on every side; it may be on the bare hill behind it is, or it may be in the heart of the wood.' The best edition is *The Secret Commonwealth*, ed. Stewart Sanderson (D. S. Brewer, The Folklore Society, Cambridge & Ipswich, 1976).

48   *Pactolus*: the river in which Midas washed himself, its sands in consequence turning to gold.

60   *Cranaë*: where Paris and Helen stopped on the first evening of their flight (*Iliad* III.445); see also the end of Patrick Leigh Fermor's book, *Mani* (John Murray, London, 1950).

61   *Thomas Cavalieri*: Michaelangelo's last *inamorato*.

New and Recent Poetry from Anvil

TONY CONNOR
Metamorphic Adventures

CAROL ANN DUFFY (ed.)
Anvil New Poets 2
Sean Boustead, Colette Bryce, Kate Clanchy,
Oliver Comins, Christina Dunhill, Alice Oswald,
Richard Price, Mike Venner, John Whale

PETER DALE
Edge to Edge
NEW AND SELECTED POEMS

DICK DAVIS
Touchwood

MICHAEL HAMBURGER
Late

JAMES HARPUR
The Monk's Dream

PETER LEVI
Reed Music

IVAN V. LALIĆ
Fading
TRANSLATED FROM T
INTRODUCED BY

THOMAS N
The Lost

STANLE
Asleep in t

DENNIS O'
Qualit

PETER R
The Elegies

RUTH S
A Wonderful V